BMX

A Guide to Bicycle Motocross

D1607513

BMX

A Guide to Bicycle Motocross

CHARLES COOMBS

illustrated with photographs and diagrams

WILLIAM MORROW AND COMPANY
New York | 1983

Photo Credits

Permission for photographs is gratefully acknowledged: American Bicycle Association, pp. 87, 91; *BMX Action* Magazine, pp. 7 (Kurt Smith), 16, 23, 82 (Bob Osborn); Lee Coombs, pp. 53, 54, 59, 62, 102 bottom; Diamond Back, pp. iv, x, 17, 50; Hutch Hi-Performance, p. 14; MCS, pp. 18, 19; National Bicycle League, pp. 5 (J.B. McCollister), 11, 72 both, 74, 90, 94; NBL, *Bicycles Today*, pp. 76, 79 bottom; Schwinn, pp. 4 top, 12, 43; Skyway, p. 38; Jim Veltman, pp. 79 top, 99. All other photographs by the author.

Printed in the United States of America.

10 9 8 7 6 5

Library of Congress Cataloging in Publication Data
Coombs, Charles Ira, 1914-   BMX, a guide to bicycle motocross. Includes index. Summary: A guide to bicycle motocross with details on choosing and repairing BMX bikes, trick riding, and successful racing strategies. 1. Bicycle motocross—Juvenile literature. [1. Bicycle motocross. 2. Bicycle racing] I. Title. II. Title: B.M.X., a guide to bicycle motocross.
GV1049.3.C66   1983   796.6   82-20904
ISBN 0-688-01867-X

ACKNOWLEDGMENT

One of the biggest delights in exploring and then writing about interesting and exciting new subjects is the enthusiasm encountered wherever I go to watch, talk with, and shoot pictures of young people having fun. Perhaps that is one reason why the response was quick and complete no matter where I turned for help on BMX biking—from the presidents of bicycle companies to the kids I stopped on the street.

It's not easy to single anyone out. After all, people from Schwinn, Huffy, Raleigh, Diamond Back, Torker, Skyway, Murray Ohio, Red Line Engineering, and other names familiar to BMXers were quick to help with both information and illustrations.

Officials of the National Bicycle League (NBL) and the American Bicycle Association (ABA), the two major bicycling organizations in the United States, were most cooperative. I particularly want to thank John Badia, who edits the fine NBL monthly publication called *Bicycles Today*, for keeping in touch and cheerfully providing both factual and pictorial help.

Closer to home, there was Ron Jacobson, an active cyclist and the proprietor and master mechanic at the Westlake Cyclery. Not only did Ron give me good counsel but he lent assorted bikes for purposes of pictures and fieldwork.

Then there was Gerry Humphrey, who, when he's not in school, works for Ron. Gerry not only sells and repairs bikes, he races them. He really knows what BMXing is all about. Among other things, he checked the manuscript carefully for errors or misconceptions. If you run across any mistakes, don't blame Gerry, blame me. I made some last-minute revisions that he didn't know about, but then, new and innovative as it is, BMX activity is constantly changing. So don't look too avidly for hard-and-fast rules. They are inclined to change as the sport does.

Just enjoy yourself and your bike, and the whole world of BMXing will open to you.

For their cheerful help, I want to thank the few mentioned above and the many who, although anonymous, pitched in wholeheartedly to make the writing of this book both pleasant and possible.

Charles "Chick" Coombs
Westlake Village, California
1983

CONTENTS

Motocross riders have fun on small, durable,
stripped-down bicycles.

ONE

The Beginnings

Bicycle motocross, or simply BMX, is a cycling sport popular with young people seeking the most in two-wheeled fun and excitement. BMX began as a direct imitation of the motorcycling sport in which throttle-twisting daredevils race over hills, jump ravines, and slog through swamps at their roaring, tire-spinning motorcycle motocross (MX) meets. Now, however, bicycle motocross runs on its own two wheels, as it were.

This sport uses specially built low-slung, sturdy bicycles designed and manufactured to hold up under riding abuse that would destroy a standard touring bicycle. The whole concept of BMX is founded on the desire of cyclists to push themselves and their bikes to the very edge of excitement, skill, and endurance.

The bicycling version of motocross is well suited to young, energetic riders, both boys and girls. Anyone who can reach the pedals can ride a BMX bike. BMX demands a high degree of physical fitness and muscular coordination, as well as the ability to make quick decisions. It is less ear-splitting, much less expensive, and infinitely safer than motorcycle racing. It provides healthy, usually strenuous exercise and does not pollute or unduly tear up the terrain. And you do not need a driver's license to ride a BMX bike.

Bicycle motocross did not appear suddenly upon the scene of wheeled sports complete with skilled riders, durable vehicles, and a firm set of rules, however. It began slowly in the late 1960s on the West Coast among those seeking to emulate motorcyclists while still on foot-powered bicycles. Usually being too young for motorized competition and unable to afford expensive gas-burning, knobby-tired dirt bikes, these budding daredevils began to test their skill and nerve on their regular touring bikes.

They started by doing simple wheelies, a trick that is performed by hauling back on the handlebars in order to bring the front wheel up and then balancing on the rear wheel. Before long these riders became amazingly skilled at cruising around for quite some distance on the rear wheel alone. Tiring of that, they then began jumping off curbs, soaring over stumps, and laying their bikes down in fender-bending slides. Many standard street bicycles ended up with bent wheels, snapped pedals, burst tires, fractured forks, or broken frames as these overly ambitious, daring cyclers pretended they were charging around on rugged, fully horsepowered motorcycles. The bikes simply could not take such abuse.

Then one manufacturer came out with a sturdily built small-wheeled bicycle. It sported motorcycle-type high-rise handlebars, had no fancy gearshifts and little if any fenders, and was equipped with tough, knobby-treaded tires. Well braced and reinforced for added strength, it was a bike that at least helped support the daredevil fantasies of these young cyclers. To an ever increasing degree, bicycles were becoming airborne vehicles.

Then, about 1970, a very popular youth movie on motorcycle motocross swept the country. The producer inserted into it a short section of film showing kids on small-wheeled, stripped-down bicycles directly imitating the motorcyclists. Never before had the general public seen such bicycling action. It looked exciting, like real fun. Young people across the country, but particularly on the West Coast where it had all begun, plunged into the new style of bicycling. BMX was born.

However, there were not nearly enough rugged bikes to satisfy the growing demand. Since the standard street tour-

The bicycle
motocross rider does
a pedal-powered
version—

—of his
motorcycling
forerunner.

ing types simply could not hold up under the punishment
of dirt riding, a few motorcycle shops began to weld together small rugged frames, beefing up the front forks and
strengthening the rear stays. They mounted the assembly
on twenty-inch balloon-tired wheels that were commonly
used on midsized street bikes. Some shop mechanics
added regular motorcycle handlebars and a firm, narrow
racing seat. They did away with everything fancy. The
keys to production were strength, durability, and, insofar
as possible, lightness.

Small frame, large tires, and a tall seat post typify
a BMX racing machine.

Any jump is fair game to the BMX trickster.

In effect, these stable small bikes were made to fly as well as to ride. Eager young daredevils sought them out and immediately began to take on the highest curbs and roughest trails. This off-street sport gained popularity in almost direct proportion to the number of bikes that were available. Soon several large motorcycle companies set up separate assembly lines solely for the production of BMX-type bikes.

At this time, the new style of bicycle riding was still just unorganized neighborhood fun. Any obstacle that could be jumped over, ridden through, or dodged around became fair game for testing one's pedaling prowess. However, all too often some young motocrosser became careless, both of private property and of his or her own safety.

To prevent total and dangerous chaos by kids on flying bicycles, parents and some civic-minded adults began exploring ways to organize the activity and make it safer without spoiling the fun. Some kind of specially planned and laid-out obstacle course was needed in order to get the racers off the streets. Rules and regulations were considered.

Although exact times and origins are dim, during 1971 and 1972 a few crudely constructed tracks appeared in some states in the Southeast and Southwest. Complete with jumps, bumps, turns, twists, and sometimes even mudholes, the dirt courses provided arenas wherein young

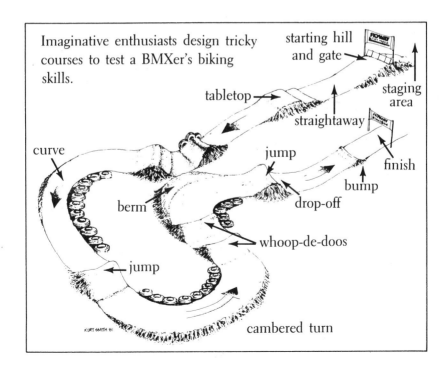

Imaginative enthusiasts design tricky courses to test a BMXer's biking skills.

riders could test their mettle and pit their muscles and riding skills against one another in safety. Often, as incentive, a trophy or award awaited them beyond the finish line.

Soon such established bicycle riding and racing bodies as the National Bicycle League (NBL), the American Bicycle Association (ABA), the National Bicycle Association (NBA), and the United Bicycle Racers (UBR) recognized the growing popularity and importance of bicycle motocross. Each of these institutions began organizing BMX activities. Things did not always run smoothly. Separate sanctioning bodies had a tendency to go their own way and set up their own rules and regulations. This caused some confusion among the young racers, who were faced with one set of guidelines and operating standards at one track and another somewhere else.

Although it still leaned heavily on its motorcycling heritage and had not yet really become a separate, fully developed sport, by 1976 BMX racing generally had settled into a basic pattern. Certain accepted guidelines were formulated to apply solely to the new style bicycling competition. To establish a standard, the basic BMX bike could not have wheels over twenty inches in diameter. This was the size wheel usually found on street bikes built for preteenagers. No specific criteria were set up for construction of the new brand of bikes, but the very fact that poorly built vehicles would quickly deteriorate under the rough treatment of motocross action established certain norms. In order to remain in business, manufacturers had to design, test, and continually upgrade their BMX bikes.

As the bikes became more radical in design, their riders rode them in ever more radical ways. And the very word "radical," shortened to "Rad," became a favored word in motocross language, denoting anything risky or tricky.

Spills and accidents increased in direct proportion to how radically the bikes were ridden. Injuries followed. Although not usually serious, they were plentiful, with a scattering of cuts, abrasions, loose teeth, and a fair share of broken bones.

Safety measures were needed and a veritable survival kit emerged. Today, in order to participate in officially sanctioned BMX races, a cyclist is required to wear a helmet, protective clothing, and shoes, and may choose other optional safety gear to help prevent injuries. As track competition increases in speed and daring, regulations are updated to keep the sport safe.

'In order to make the competition fair to all, bicycle motocross racers are separated into classes. Occasionally they are grouped by size and weight of the riders. However, it has become almost standard procedure to divide BMX racers into groups according to age and experience. Starting at, say, age five and under, the classes progress upward through six-, seven-, eight-, or nine-year-olds, and on up beyond the teens; and since BMX is family fun, adult races are staged at some meets.

The age breakdown depends somewhat on who is putting on the racing meet and what rules are being followed. At least, a five-year-old isn't expected to compete against a fifteen-year-old.

Consideration also is given to the amount of experience a racer has had. If you never before have participated in organized BMX racing, you are classed as a beginner and race against other beginners within your own age range. With a little experience you move up to the novice class. After you have won a few trophies you graduate to expert class.

Girls compete in their own races on the same track used by the boys. They, too, are separated into age groups in order to even out the rivalry. Although girls' races are known in motocross language as powder puff events, they are just as serious and generate just as much excitement as any other events in a meet. By mutual agreement girls occasionally pit themselves against boys.

Girls compete as vigorously as boys in BMX racing events.

Finally, there are the pros. All the professionals come up through the ranks of beginners, novices, and experts; but to be a professional a racer must be at least sixteen years old. In comparison to the thousands of amateur BMXers, the ranks of the pros are very small. Just like the professionals in any sport, BMX pros race for both trophies and prize money. They might even pick up additional earnings by lending their names to an advertising campaign or otherwise plugging someone's product. Or pros may plaster their bikes, helmets, and clothes with stickers, decals, and patches and receive some sort of recompense for that. BMX racing is a tough way to make a living, but a select few manage to do it, for a short length of time.

If you aspire to becoming a pro and are one of the few who make it, you probably will need a sponsor to provide equipment and help pay expenses as you travel from meet to meet. The sponsor may be the owner of a local bike shop or a dealer of bicycle parts and products. If you are really topnotch, you may be picked to join a sponsored team, called a factory team. But you don't really have to be a pro, since factory teams also include amateurs.

There are races for both amateurs and professionals.

By the late 1970s bicycle motocross racing had become quite well organized, and tremendously popular and widespread. It took on an image of its own, almost completely shedding its identity with motorcycling. Indeed, some enthusiasts even forsook their more expensive, complicated, and dangerous motorcycles for BMX bikes.

By the beginning of the 1980s bicycle motocross was in full swing. Its popularity spread rapidly from coast to coast, border to border, and spilled over into Canada, England, and the European mainland. It took hold in the Orient, where so many of the best bikes and parts are manufactured. It spread to Australia, Africa, and just about every other place on the globe where people ride bicycles. Late in 1978, in order to handle worldwide aspects of the burgeoning sport, the International Bicycle Motocross Federation (IBMXF) was established in the Netherlands.

However, what is considered legitimate or officially sanctioned bicycle motocross racing accounts for only a small segment of BMX biking. For every boy or girl who registers to ride, pays a fee, and races for trophies under organized conditions, literally thousands of others use their BMX bikes for informal fun.

When not riding to school, running errands, or otherwise making practical use of their BMX-designed bikes, they use them in whatever radical fashion they can think of. They ride freestyle and do wheelies, as well as jump, dodge, slide, or slog. They ride wherever they can find a little open space. They just thrash about—and that is what they call it, thrashing—for sheer fun and daring.

No matter whether they ride for the challenge of competition, or simply to put their bikes and themselves through the paces, young people the world over are sharing in the delight and excitement of bicycle motocross action.

A couple of young racers duel it out on a wooded track.

TWO

The Machines

The popularity of bicycle motocross activities spawned an entirely new species of bicycle. To a BMXer, a bike is no longer something simply to pedal around on. This rider needs a bike that can endure the punishment of rough usage accented by violent skidding, jumping, and crashing. He or she also will be directing much effort to defying gravity while performing all sorts of breathless two-wheeled aerobatics. In order to do all this, while hoping to escape mishap and breakdowns, a motocross cyclist needs a bike that is light enough to fly, yet has the strength and stability of a superjet's landing gear.

That is why BMX bikes are built smaller and sturdier than stock department-store vehicles. Yet, they have an appealing appearance and are sufficiently versatile to ride to school, pedal to a fishing stream, or serve any other transportation function that a standard bicycle can. Motocross bikes are designed mostly for young riders; an adult is seldom seen pedaling around on one.

BMX bikes are largely antigravity machines.

Most standard street bikes can get by with a fairly soft aluminum or "mild" steel frame. A BMX machine is made of tougher materials. High-tensile steel or heat-treated aluminum alloys often work out satisfactorily. A much favored material for the better BMX bikes is tempered chrome molybdenum, or chrome-moly steel, usually carrying the code number 4130. It is made into such heavily stressed components as frames, forks, handlebar stems, and seat posts.

The basic BMX bicycle.

Manganese molybdenum (mang-moly or magaloy) is almost as strong as chrome-moly and has excellent welding properties; but it is less available. Indeed, one might go to titanium, which is lighter and stronger than any of the others. But titanium is extremely expensive, and so not often used.

The bicycle frame is the foundation of any bike. It usually is made up of a basic front triangle composed of a horizontal top tube, a downward-angling down tube, and a fairly vertical-rising seat mast. These three basic pieces are ordinarily cut from 1-inch- or 1¼-inch-diameter tubing stock. Their ends are butted together and welded to form the main triangle. Metal braces, or gussets, are sometimes added to the corners to increase strength.

A rack of BMX frames.

Behind the seat mast another double triangle is made up of a pair of chain stays and seat stays. These form a fork-like assembly that holds the rear wheel and sprocket in place. Many chain and seat stays are single loops of tubing rather than separate pieces. Drop-outs, or axle slots, are located where the stays merge so the rear wheel can be quickly removed or the chain tension adjusted by sliding the axle forward or backward in the slot.

Frames come in a wide variety of sizes and shapes. A BMX frame is smaller than the frame of a touring bicycle. It has a squeezed or flattened diamond-shaped design in order to raise the bottom bracket hanger higher from the ground. This allows for longer pedal cranks, while still providing for a safe clearance of the pedals from the

Strong, precision welding is essential to a good frame.

ground. Long cranks add getaway power, or torque, for the pedaler.

Normally, when you first get into BMX riding you purchase your specialized bike fully assembled and ready to ride. As you gain experience and want a more sprightly vehicle, you may prefer to start with a basic frame and build your machine with an assortment of separate components purchased through dealers or a bike shop. In doing this, you choose a set of strong tubular front forks that are lightweight yet able to withstand the shock of hard landings. They, too, have drop-out slots for easy adjustment or change of the front wheel. The forks must be properly raked, or slanted forward, so the bike steers properly. The angle of the headset tube, the short forward part of the frame that contains the handlebar and fork bearings, also helps determine the rake of the forks and affects steering.

If the forks rake too far forward, the front wheel tends to go over on its side when you turn your handlebars, causing you to spin out on a curve. If there is too little rake, your bike becomes overly sensitive to the touch and may flop you forward in a high-speed turn. Any bike shop will help you check the angle of rake, which should be about eighteen to twenty-two degrees from the vertical. Then, too, there is nothing like taking a trial spin on the machine to help you determine how a bike responds to the handlebars.

BMX handlebars are usually of a somewhat moderated and lowered high-rise, steerhorn-shaped variety. Due to the rough treatment they get, handlebars should be reinforced by a straight or V-bent cross brace welded at the middle. The handlebars should be a comfortable width, with the tips of the soft rubber end grips approximately two feet apart but not over the maximum twenty-eight inches allowed. Aluminum alloy or chrome-moly handlebars are most commonly used.

Since there is much tugging, pushing, and jerking on BMX handlebars, they must be clamped firmly in a special superstrong stem, or gooseneck. This fits into the frame's headset tube, which also supports the front forks. Unlike the stem on a stock bike, the double-clamp BMX stem often has up to four bolts that grip the handlebars and prevent them from twisting or slipping under the most jarring usage.

Nothing is more important, of course, than the wheels of your bike. Official BMX racing wheels are not supposed to be over twenty inches in diameter, which has long been a standard size used on midsized bicycles. Very young riders of, say, seven and under normally race on sixteen-inch minibike wheels. Larger beach cruisers or mountain trail bikes, which can be stripped down and beefed up as BMX racing machines, use twenty-four- or twenty-six-inch wheels. Such bikes are suitable for larger, heavier, and perhaps older riders to thrash about or race with. These competitors are sometimes the parents of younger contestants out sharing the fun together, probably in separate races.

Wheel rims usually are made of steel, alloyed aluminum, tightly compressed nylon, or a thermoplastic material. Any material is acceptable, as long as the wheel is strong enough to hold the spokes and survive the poundings it gets. BMX wheels often have a few extra heavy-gauge spokes for additional fortification, perhaps thirty-two or thirty-six spokes instead of the more customary twenty-eight. However, despite precautions and extra strengthening of the wheel, bent and twisted rims, plus snapped and tangled spokes, are common sights around BMX racetracks.

One method of avoiding spoke problems is to equip your bike with mag-type wheels. These, too, can be made of aluminum alloy or some strong plastic material. Spokeless and usually molded in one piece of brightly colored material, mag wheels are durable and not easily warped or

Mag or spoke wheels are usually a matter of personal preference.

crushed. Usually heavier and less popular than lightweight steel-spoked wheels, the mag wheels are nonetheless showing up more and more frequently on everyday street bikes as well as on BMX racing machines.

Wheel rims are designed to accept heavy-duty BMX tires. Except for being smaller in size, a bicycle motocross tire is quite similar to the tire used on a lightweight dirt-riding motorcycle. It has a knobby or gnarly tread that will bite into the loose dirt, sand, or mud of trails or tracks. Most treads wrap part way around the sidewall to provide a

Knobby-treaded tires grip into dirt paths or tracks.

good grip on the terrain when a rider lays the bike over on a high-speed turn.

Bicycle tires are made to fit all sizes of wheels and are usually 1.75 inches or 2.125 inches in cross-section diameter. Whereas the sixteen-inch wheels are used on many of the smaller bikes pedaled by young people under seven or eight years old, by far the majority of BMX bikes are equipped with twenty-inch wheels. The most common sized BMX tires are 20 × 1.75 and 20 × 2.125. Larger twenty-four- and twenty-six-inch tires fit the bigger cruisers, or open-wheel racers, as some call them.

The younger riders usually use the same sized smaller diameter (1.75-inch) tires on both front and rear wheels. The more experienced racers often put the larger (2.125-inch) tire on the front to provide better steering traction and the smaller tire on the rear power wheel for lightness and ease of pedaling.

Critical to any bike, of course, is the drive train—the parts that make the vehicle go. The drive train starts at the pedals. The pedals attach to the cranks, which spin the large front sprocket, or chainwheel. The chainwheel drives the continuous chain that turns the rear sprocket. The rear sprocket rotates the back wheel. It is a simple and straight-forward system for transferring foot power to wheel power.

The power end of a BMX bike.

The pedals on a BMX bike are invariably of the rattrap style. Each is made up of a simple cage mounted on a free-turning spindle. The so-called foot-fitting cage usually is notched or equipped with nonskid studs or teeth to prevent the soft soles of your shoes from slipping off during the wild skirmish of racing action. You do not use toe clips on BMX pedals. By the very nature of motocross riding, one moment you may have to thrust a foot to the ground to prevent crashing, and the next moment you go back to pedaling furiously. So you must be able to move your feet freely on or off the pedals, which is not possible with toe clips. Your pedals should be no wider than necessary for comfort and a secure fit. The wider the pedals, the more chance of their digging into the dirt when you lean your bike over into a turn.

The rotating cranks to which your pedals attach usually are a bit longer on a BMX bike than on a standard street bike. From 170 to 180 millimeters (about 7 inches) is the norm. Small riders may use 150-millimeter (approximately 6-inch) cranks. The longer the cranks, the more immediate power, or torque, you can produce, and the quicker you can accelerate. However, you must also have good leg muscles to get the longer cranks turning. So it is usually best to strike a happy medium between short cranks that demand faster pedaling and long cranks that demand extra strength.

The cranks on a BMX bike must be very strong in order to withstand the abuse from collisions, loss of control during a skid, or plowing into a barrier. BMX cranks are usually sturdier than those on stock bicycles. They can be made of heat-treated aluminum alloy, high-tensile steel, or the highly favored chrome-moly. A few riders even seem able to afford titanium.

Left and right cranks are connected by a spindle that is supported by bearings set into the round bottom bracket located at the bottom of the frame where the seat mast and down tube come together. Some one-piece crank sets are forged from a single metal bar and do not require a connecting spindle. However, they, too, turn in bottom bracket bearings.

(Left) Muscle power that drives the bike focuses at the bottom hanger of the frame.

(Below) Rear hub and freewheel sprocket convert chain drive to wheel power.

On some models the front chainwheel is built right into the crank set. On others a simple starlike "spider" is used. With a spider you can choose and attach different-sized steel or composition chainwheels having varying numbers of teeth, thereby changing the gearing of your bicycle. Depending on their sizes, front chainwheels may have from less than forty to more than fifty teeth in them. This is in contrast to the smaller rear sprocket, which may have some thirteen to twenty-two teeth. Choosing the right-sized sprockets for varying tracks and racing conditions goes a long way toward winning races.

A large chainwheel with a small rear sprocket produces a high, or hard, gear ratio. A high ratio requires fewer pedal revolutions to take you where you want to go. But it also demands more strength to get you there.

A small chainwheel with a large rear sprocket provides a low, or soft, gear ratio. This makes pedaling up a hill easier, but you have to crank faster on level ground to build up and maintain speed.

You can use any combination of front and rear sprockets that works best for you. But, under racing conditions, the person who has practiced most and is in the best physical condition is more apt to win the race than an opponent who struggles with a pocket computer trying to determine which gear ratio leads to victory.

You should know something about gear ratios, however, for they affect the proper running of a race when all other factors are equal. To determine what your gear ratio is, you divide the number of teeth in the larger chainwheel by the number of teeth in the rear sprocket, also called a freewheel on bikes not equipped with coaster brakes. For example, if you have a 44-tooth chainwheel and divide it by a 16-tooth freewheel, expressed as $^{44}/_{16}$, your gear ratio is 2.75. So every time you pedal the chainwheel around for a full revolution, you rotate the rear sprocket, and the back wheel that it turns, 2¾ times, or 2.75 wheel revolutions. Just remember, the higher the ratio the harder it is to accelerate but the faster you can go once you are underway. The lower the ratio, the easier it is to get moving out of the gate, but the faster you have to churn your legs to maintain speed. By and large, most racers feel that they have better control over their bikes by using a fairly low gear ratio. Unless you are deeply into BMX racing strategy, chances are you probably will stick with the midrange gear ratio that your bike comes with.

Now consider the all-important chain that ties the drive train together. The continuous loop of chain consists of a series of carefully engineered links that fit precisely over the sprocket teeth. Each link is made up of two side plates and two rollers, held together by a pair of rivetlike pins.

Some chains are factory closed and available in varying sizes to fit different drive trains. Other chains have master links that can be taken apart so you can adjust the chain's length by adding or removing links. The most common chain link sizes are ⅛ inch × ½ inch. The ⅛ signifies the thickness of the sprocket teeth that the chain must fit. The ½ denotes the distance between the link pins. A good quality chain is essential if you expect top service from your bike.

A foot-operated coaster brake is perfectly acceptable on a bike you intend to use primarily for street, trail, or free-style riding. Some racing bikes, too, still use coaster brakes. A major drawback in using a coaster brake is that the rider has to backpedal about a half stroke in order to activate the brake. Then, to accelerate forward again, he or she has to make up that half-stroke reverse rotation before the pedals take hold. That takes time, perhaps a half second. Not much, perhaps, but many a race is won or lost by a few milliseconds.

So, by far the majority of competitive bikers rely on hand-operated, rim-squeezing caliper brakes. Some use a single caliper brake on the rear wheel, where it is most needed. Others mount brakes on both front and rear wheels, finding they can obtain better slowing or stopping control by using either or both as the situation requires.

A rear-wheel caliper brake is most commonly used.

With a caliper brake the BMXer uses a freely turning rear sprocket instead of the complicated and less effective coaster brake. This simple, trouble-free, frictionless free-wheel is highly desirable for smooth running.

Forget gearshifts on BMX bikes. Very few racing machines have them. There is little time, opportunity, or need during a short, half-minute, high-speed motocross race to be concerned with shifting gears. Thus, nearly all BMX bikes are one-speed machines.

Long ago BMX bikes abandoned the use of any sort of springs or shock-absorbing suspension systems that added comfort to a ride. The flexibilty detracted from the BMX bike's sensitivity and its ability to accelerate without first wasting the split second it took for the springs to snap back to their neutral position. In a race a rider cannot afford this time, no matter how short it might be. Solid-framed, so-called hardtail bikes that respond instantly to pedal pressures took over and remain overwhelmingly in command of BMX action.

A seat, or saddle, is important. Yet, during the action of a motocross race your rump is off the saddle more than on it. You stand on the pedals, or slide forward or back away from the saddle to adjust your balance according to the needs of the maneuver you perform. So, a BMX saddle usually is a hard, narrow, racing type. It perches atop a long, hard steel post that protrudes perhaps a foot or so up out of the hollow seat mast, depending upon your size. Of course, the seat post is adjustable to your comfort and is held firmly in place by a strong clamp. Some want the seat low and out of the way; others prefer it high and use it more. Probably the most widely accepted measure is to set the seat so that your knee bends only slightly when your foot touches the pedal at its lowest point. It's an individual choice, with comfort being the main object.

You also will want to consider the appearance of your motocross bike. As with so many modern-day sports, bright colors illuminate all areas of motocross biking. Although perhaps not considered a color shade, much bright nickel and chrome finishing is used on many bike parts, such as handlebars, wheels, forks, and sometimes even the frames. On the other hand, most bikes display an assortment of shiny anodized colors or bright epoxy paint finishes. It is probably no accident that the pride reflected by a clean, neatly painted, spiffed-up bike is the same pride that helps win races.

Spongelike polyurethane-foam protective pads are commonly used, and frequently required, to help cushion a rider against injury. They are lightweight, usually brightly colored, and often carry some product name or advertising slogan. Inexpensive additions, they are attached to the top tube, the handlebar cross brace, and the protruding handlebar stem in order to soften the impact when the cyclist bashes against the frame. If you are going to do any radical riding—and surely you will—don't fail to pad your bike.

Decals, stickers, and patches are as much a part of BMX motocross as they are in most other sporting activities. Bikes, riders, and tracks are ablaze with bright, appealing colors.

And, of course, a number plate is the one thing that really identifies a competitive BMX bike. Mounted on the handlebars, it comes in a variety of shapes and color combinations. Its one function is to display the numbers assigned the cyclist for a particular racing meet.

A sprightly, durable bicycle not only gives you a feeling of pride but also helps you to excel in BMX activities.

THREE

Choosing a Bike

Shopping for a BMX bicycle can become frustrating unless you have a pretty good idea of what you are looking for. Once you have a fair knowledge of the parts that make up a bike, consider the total machine.

When fully assembled, motocross bikes vary considerably in weight, and weight is important. Lightness plus strength are always major factors to be sought. A minibike used by the smallest riders may weigh fourteen or fifteen pounds. Somewhat older, heavier, and more muscular cyclists usually pedal a bike weighing twenty-three to thirty pounds, or even a bit more. The pros, who usually rate the finest and most expensive bikes, constructed of the best lightweight materials, race with regular-sized bikes that weigh between twenty and twenty-six pounds.

By and large, try to find a bike that is lightweight enough to make the best use of your muscle power yet solid enough to endure rough treatment.

Due to a choice of carefully engineered components

that are made of the most durable yet lightweight materials, a BMX bicycle usually is more expensive than a
standard street bike. You can purchase a fairly good, but
not really competitive, motocross-style bike for around one
hundred and twenty dollars. For a real trackworthy charger
you may have to invest two or three hundred dollars. The
price can go above five or six hundred dollars. That sum is
quite steep for all but a select few really dedicated or perhaps sponsored racers.

A twenty-six-inch beach cruiser contrasts markedly with a twenty-
inch BMX racer, but both are competitive.

There is a wide variety of BMX bikes from which to choose.

Once you have a fair concept of the parts that make up a BMX bike, it is time to browse around the bike shops to see how they are put together. Note the difference in the quality of components between the less expensive, the moderately priced, and the topline vehicles. See how the rough, lumpy spot welding on cheaper bikes gives way to smooth, continuous beaded welding on the better vehicles.

Check how smoothly and truly the wheels turn on the bike. On a poorer quality machine you may detect a slight wobble or a grittiness in the all-important wheel bearings. Inferior ones may surge and grind. Good bearings will roll silently and steadily.

Unless the bike is equipped with a coaster brake—and

some good BMX bikes still are—work the caliper brakes to be sure they respond quickly to your gentle pressure on the brake lever or levers mounted on the handlebars. See if the brake shoes press equally on both sides of the wheel rim and spring away slightly clear of the rim when you release the handle. The smoothness of the leverage action gives an indication of their quality.

Check the gooseneck holding the handlebars. It must have a sure grip, or the handlebars will twist and swivel when you crash or tug on them during a ride. Many fine handlebar stems have more than one tightening screw.

The rattrap pedals should be strongly constructed yet lightweight. Metal cages are probably more durable, yet

Rattrap pedals are durable yet lightweight.

quite a few plastic and composition cages hold up well.

See that the chain has the sheen and solid feel of good quality.

Look closely at the finish on the bike. You don't need sharp eyes to detect the difference between a hastily sprayed single-coat paint job and a carefully layered smooth epoxy finish. Cracked paint around a joint might indicate a fractured weld. Also look closely around decals or stickers to be sure they don't camouflage a flaw. Inspect nickel or chrome plating for pits or peeling.

When you have become fairly expert at knowing what to look for and think you can tell a good component from an inferior one, talk to the dealer or shop owner. He or she can be of valuable help during a purchase and an essential aide whenever your bike requires adjustment or repair. A forthright dealer or shopman will ask you questions to determine what type of BMX riding you have in mind. He or she will also consider your size, spirit, and ambitions before making recommendations.

Consider the complete package when you are deliberating whether or not to buy. Be sure your bike has proper reflectors if you are going to use it for street riding. And add a light for night use. With the proper amount of searching and testing, you should be able to find a BMX bike to fit both your budget and riding skills.

Of course, you can look for bargains at swap meets, flea markets, garage sales, or police auctions. You can check the classified ads in your newspaper. Just realize that you usually take whatever you get in such transactions "as is." No returns, refunds, or adjustments.

Anyway, whether you are buying or just looking, it is well worth your while to acquaint yourself with the variety of BMX bicycles that have emerged in recent years. They have been designed and engineered to survive the hard usage in which young riders take such delight. Whether for neighborhood sport, dirt-trail riding, or racing competition, the BMX-style bike is a low-slung, sturdy sporting machine built to fit the needs of young people pursuing the fun and challenge of bicycle motocross.

FOUR

Preparing to Ride

Once you have your bike, you can concentrate on what you need to do to get the best use and most pleasure from it. Most BMX bike riders are enthusiasts who just enjoy thrashing around. Others, of course, set out to locate an official BMX track so they can pit their speed and riding skills against others of similar age and experience.

However, whether you are bent on thrashing or racing, you must consider what to wear for both comfort and safety. For street riding you can get by with almost any type of clothes. Chances are that most of the time you will wear the same clothes that you wear to school. Jeans, slacks, or other style pants, and an ordinary blouse, sweater, or tee shirt are almost standard biking uniforms.

You should, however, consider certain sensible precautions whenever you ride your bike, particularly if you intend to put it through a few tricks. After all, even when you are riding calmly to school, seldom will you be able to

Most riders thrash around in everyday street clothes.

resist the temptation to jump a curb, wheelie past a barking dog, or skid to a rubber-burning stop at the bike rack.

If possible, you should wear pants that are tight in the legs. Even chain guards will not effectly keep oil or grease off floppy pant legs. If you remove the chain guard, you can almost certainly count on loose pant legs getting chewed up by sprockets and chain. Yet, many do remove the guard in order to lighten up the bike or prevent a loose guard from tangling in a wheel. Of course, you can use clips or rubber bands around the legs, but not many riders want to fuss with them. Tight trouser legs are the simplest solution to the problems of keeping clean and clear of machinery.

The very nature of thrashing around and performing freestyle stunts on a BMX bike virtually guarantees that now and then you will take a spill, or "crash and burn," as BMXers say. Therefore, long sleeves are needed to protect your arms from assorted bruises, scratches, and cuts.

Tight pants legs and comfortable shoes fit most BMX riding activities.

You really do not need specialized shoes for riding a motocross bike. Some cyclists advocate high leather shoes for the best protection for feet and ankles. They should have soft rubber soles that grip the rattrap pedals. But not many everyday riders wear leather shoes. Tennis shoes are much more comfortable and popular, although they afford less protection than leather. Running and jogging shoes that have sufficiently soft soles for clinging securely to rattrap pedals make good motocross riding shoes. Laced shoes are more secure on your feet than slip-ons. Whatever you choose to wear, just be sure that your footwear is lightweight, so your energy goes toward moving the pedals not the shoes. Wear heavy socks to keep your legs and ankles from getting banged up. Bare feet, thongs, or sandals simply won't do if you have any regard for the care and safety of your feet.

Even in neighborhood biking you should wear some kind of protective headgear, particularly if you ride where there is any automobile traffic or if you intend to jump over stumps or spin your bike around in reverse skids. You can wear a motorcycling helmet, although you may find it too heavy.

You are required to wear a helmet when you race. BMX helmets are fabricated of lightweight but excep-

Head and face protection is the best insurance against injury.

tionally strong fiberglass with a padded nylon-covered liner that fits snugly over your head. The helmet must have a strong chin strap to hold it securely in place at all times, whether during a jump or when tangling in a crash.

Many helmets have strong mouthguards built into them. Others have fasteners to which you can attach a mouthguard. In either case, such guards are cheap tooth insurance.

Colors, of course, are optional, and come in all rainbow hues. On top of that, many racers plaster their helmets with decals and stickers usually handed out by someone trying to advertise a product.

Above all, the helmet must be strong and secure

enough, as well as properly fitted, to pass a race official's close inspection.

Helmets vary greatly in style, quality, cost, and durability. It is a good idea to check with your bicycle dealer for the model best suited to your size, safety, and riding conditions. The smart biker always wears a helmet whenever or wherever he or she rides. All in all, you must dress to protect yourself from the risks you intend to take.

While riding, you must observe all safety rules. On a two-way street always ride on the right side of the road. That is, ride with the flow of traffic, never against it. Remember how lightweight and vulnerable both you and your bike are. Don't get into arguments over who has the right-of-way; yield to all other vehicles and, indeed, even

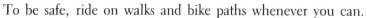

To be safe, ride on walks and bike paths whenever you can.

to pedestrians. Stick to whatever bike lanes your community has laid out. Unless it is prohibited, you are safer riding on unoccupied sidewalks.

When on the streets, use the proper hand signals—left forearm up to turn right, straight out to turn left, and down to slow or stop. Beware of cars turning into or backing out of driveways. If you ride at night, be sure your BMX bike is equipped with a good light and plenty of reflectors. Wear light-colored, highly visible clothing.

Above all, keep alert, watch any and all traffic around you, and ride defensively. Buffer yourself with plenty of open space in all directions.

Never ride double. Not only are small BMX bikes ill-suited to it but riding two people on a bike is illegal and an invitation to disaster.

These are some of the considerations you should make when you intend to ride around the neighborhood and local trails on your BMX machine. When you compete in organized motocross races under official sanction, you discover that the restrictions on dress and safety are no longer optional. You abide by the established standards or you simply don't race.

The clothing and accessories you adorn yourself with for BMX racing competition bear little resemblance to the casual, everyday trappings you can get by with for informal thrashing around. Your racing jersey may be made of almost any material but must have long sleeves. Simple crew neck tee shirts are popular.

Dedicated BMX racers wear special protective pants called leathers, patterned after those worn by motorcyclists. However, seldom are they made of real animal hide. Not only is genuine leather expensive and difficult to clean or mend, but a hard-pedaling bicyclist could quickly overheat in leather pants. So BMX leathers usually are made of strongly knit nylon or other durable fabric. They fit tightly around the hips and legs without hindering free movement in any direction. The legs are zippered or closed with Velcro fasteners to keep them snug and away from the moving parts of the bike.

Some leathers are padded, particularly in the knees and hips. If pads are not built in, you can use regular basketball knee and elbow pads, worn inside or outside your racing pants or jersey, although inside and out of the way is generally preferred. Perhaps you can even find a used pair of football hip pads to wear. Proper padding is essential to protect against the inevitable banging around you will get from BMX racing. Some racing suits are one-piece outfits not unlike tight-fitting jumpsuits. They usually have built-in pads at the elbows, knees, and hips.

Properly dressed for competition.

As in so many other types of sports, you find BMX bikes, clothing, and accessories adorned with brilliant displays of mixed-and-matched colors. Bikes and clothing become signboards on which you can hang assorted decals, stickers, sew-on patches, and iron-on letters and designs.

In any event, whether you intend to ride informally around the neighborhood or plunge into some stiff racing competition, you now feel that you have a pretty good idea of what BMXing is about. You are confident that your bike will serve you well for both street riding and racing. You have chosen your colorful wearing apparel with an eye to both comfort and protection. You know the basic rules of safety. And you are eager to test your riding skills, feeling it is high time to take a spin on your new two-wheeled steed.

But hold on a minute. First things first.

Fully protected in helmet and leathers and colorfully arrayed with patches and decals, a racer does a wheelie off a berm.

FIVE

Know Your Bike

Whether you intend to use your BMX bike mainly for off-track activity or plan to challenge the champions of motocross tracks, you should thoroughly acquaint yourself with your machine. You should know how to care for it in order to keep it in top riding condition. This means keeping it clean and properly tuned. A grimy or poorly adjusted bike will not perform properly.

To do this you will need some rags and a few simple tools. Before you start to tinker with your machine, clean it up so you can see what you are doing. Go over your bike with a mild soap and water solution. Ordinary window cleaner also makes a good cleaning agent and will not damage the bike's finish. Never use gasoline on your bike, whether indoors or out. Volatile and inflammable, gasoline is much too dangerous to fool around with, and it can also ruin the finish.

If you are handy with tools, and have a mechanic's

Clean your bike
—if your pup will
let you.

knack for putting parts back together in the exact order in which you took them apart, you can tackle the tuning and lubricating yourself. However, if you lack those talents it's a good idea to leave most of the major work to the skilled hands of an experienced bicycle shop technician.

If you decide to tune and lubricate your own bike, take your time and go about it carefully. To tighten or loosen assorted nuts and bolts, you need a few box or open-end wrenches or, better still, combination wrenches that are boxed on one end and open on the other. The most handy sizes are ½, ⁹⁄₁₆, and ¹¹⁄₁₆ inch, or their metric counterparts—12, 14, and 17 mm (millimeter) respectively. These sizes are not exact substitutes, so if your bike uses metrics, a basic set of a half dozen or so metric wrenches is a worthwhile investment in order to assure the precise fit that will prevent slippage. Using the correct sizes will also prevent the corners of nuts and bolts from being rounded off.

Also, a good quality, Crescent-type, 10-inch adjustable wrench is an extremely versatile tool to have. It's good to have a pair of pliers, but you must be careful using them around a bicycle, for pliers tend to slip and chew up whatever you are working on. Channel-lock pliers are more secure, but again, if they have serrated or notched jaws, you must be careful how you use them. A couple of medium-sized screwdrivers, one to fit standard slotted screws and one for Phillips types, should be in your toolbox. A

An adjustable wrench and a puppy are very handy around a bicycle.

six-millimeter Allen screw key also is a handy item to have.

With these basic wrenches, pliers, and screwdrivers you can accomplish about 90 percent of your tuneup and adjustment work. But you may want to round out your tool kit with a small hammer or mallet and a steel punch or two for loosening stuck bearing cones and such. You may want a hacksaw to lop off the protruding ends of overlong axles.

Buy top quality tools. Not only will they last a lifetime, but they rarely slip or break and scruff up your bike.

You also need two or three simple bicycle-tire irons. These are small and properly formed to pry a tire off the rim without chewing it up or puncturing the tube, as often happens when you use a screwdriver.

Unless you have mag wheels, you need a spoke wrench. A simple T-type wrench is suited to a single gauge of spoke. But you also can get a combination wrench that fits spokes of all sizes.

A tire pressure gauge and a pump are convenient options to have. They keep you from having to traipse down to the service station or bike shop every time you want to check or inflate your tires. Besides, using high-pressure gas-station air hoses is a good way to blow a bike tire.

You should carry more than one type of lubricant. At times a can of lightweight oil is all you need. Oil does attract dirt and grime and should be used sparingly, but between greasings there's nothing wrong with oiling your pedals and chain. A drop or two of light oil also will keep your cables and brake mechanism working smoothly.

Instead of oil you might use dry silicone-based lubricants that come in spray cans. There are assorted brands, most of which work nicely on chains, pedals, or other moving parts where you normally might apply oil. And the silicone spray attracts less dirt.

However, when it comes to major bearings, such as those enclosed in wheel hubs, the bottom bracket, and the headset, oil is not the best lubricant. It is inclined to fly out of a spinning hub, get flushed out by rainwater, or simply disappear, often leaving the bearings dry. For these important bearings you should use a good grade of grease to lubricate the moving parts whenever you dismantle the bike. Rather than plain automobile-type axle grease, you might find it worthwhile to check your bike shop for a recommended bearing lubricant that is formulated particularly for bikes, resists moisture and dirt, and is long lasting.

Now then, having the basic tools and proper accessories

at hand and having cleaned your bike up a bit, you can begin checking and adjusting the machine. First of all, make sure that everything is snug. The roughness of BMX action is inclined to unsettle nuts, bolts, and screws. Shake your bike and listen for the clink or rattle of loose parts. Trace the sound and tighten whatever is causing the clatter.

Straddle the front wheel and try to wiggle the handlebars. If they are loose or wobbly, tighten the head bolt atop the handlebar stem. This wedges the expander bolt more solidly in the headset and eliminates handlebar play.

If there is any play in the front forks, loosen the locknut at the top of the headset tube. Next tighten down a little on the adjusting cup under it to take up the slack in the beveled cones that hold the bearings. When the forks feel solid but still rotate freely, snug down the locking nut.

Now get to the wheels and the power train. Turn your bike upside down so it rests on its handlebars and seat. This puts most of its parts within easy reach. This is a good time to apply a little oil to any part that seems to grind or bind.

Spin the front wheel and sight along it. See that it is properly centered between the forks. If not, loosen the wheel axle nuts and adjust the axle in the drop-out slots to

Center the wheel between the forks.

center the wheel. Also, while the wheel is spinning, look for any serpentine wobble of the rim. You can correct this by adjusting and tightening the proper spokes. However, truing up a wheel is usually a tricky process and probably best left to the expert at the bike shop.

While your attention is on the freely spinning wheel, hold a loose finger to the turning spokes. They should emit a consistent metallic *ping*. Trace down the ones that *thunk* and tighten them with your spoke wrench until they play the same tune as the others. But be careful not to overtighten the spokes or you can warp your rim and ruin a wheel. This is also a good time to check tire pressure. If the tire is soft, look for a leak and fix it according to the directions on your tire patch kit.

While the bike is upside down, clean the chain with a brush dipped in paint thinner or solvent. For a quick, clean job, spray some commercial lubricant such as WD-40 on the chain and wipe it dry. Spray it again to relubricate it. Perhaps a less thorough cleaning than you can do with a brush and can of solvent, the spray-and-wipe method, when done fairly frequently, helps keep the chain in good condition.

Check the chain tension. You do this by putting a finger under the chain about midway between the front and rear sprockets. If you can move it easily up and down

A toothbrush dipped in solvent will clean a chain.

more than a half inch, it is too loose. A loose chain may jump a sprocket during a ride and create a bad tangle, to say nothing of leaving you powerless. On the other hand, if the chain is so tight that you can't move it easily more than a quarter of an inch up and down, it may snap under the strain of a hard landing.

You can easily adjust chain tension by loosening the rear axle nuts and sliding the wheel a little forward or backward in the drop-out slots. Be sure to realign the

Adjust the chain to no more than a half inch of up-down play.

wheel, then tighten the axle nuts when everything is in place. You can use a bit of light oil on your chain, but special chain lubes are better and collect less grime.

When you are working around the chainwheel, take hold of the cranks and check them for too much play. If they rattle in the bottom bracket, you can tighten the bearing cones in much the same way that you tightened the loose headset bearings. Always tighten just enough to eliminate the wobble without binding the bearings. If you detect a gritty sound, you probably should remove the bearings, clean them in solvent, and coat them with grease. This is not a difficult job if you know what you are doing and take care not to get the parts mixed. Unless the bearings are held securely in a retainer, be careful. Loose ball bearings scatter and get lost before you can gather them up.

Now spin your pedals. Pedals usually are quite fool-proof, except when you wipe out on a corner or lose control during a jump and smash one into the ground, probably bending or breaking it. However, you should check to see that they are threaded solidly into the crank ends. Add a bit of lube to keep the pedal bearings spinning freely.

Now to the brake or brakes. If you have a coaster brake, you will find it something of a job to do more than simply

A drop of light oil keeps pedals spinning freely.

adjust the brake arm. The brake mechanism inside the rear hub is a complicated maze of cones, sleeves, rings, bearings, thrust plates, and brake shoes. Without extreme care, plus a parts chart to guide you, beware. Problems with rear hubs and coaster brakes are best left to the experts. Not that you cannot become an expert, but it takes specific training and mechanical skill.

On the other hand, caliper brakes are right out where you can get to them. They have simple adjustments. If you find it difficult to stop, you probably need to take up a little on the control cable, which has a tendency to stretch with use. You do this quite simply by loosening the bolt that holds the cable in the brake arm. Just squeeze the brake shoes to the rim, pull the cable down a little, and

Properly adjusted caliper brake shoes squeeze equally
on each side of the rim.

tighten the bolt. When you release the brake, the shoes
should spring out slightly away from the rim. By maintain-
ing a narrow clearance, you will need to squeeze the brake
lever only a fraction of an inch to activate the brake. If you
happen to have both front and rear caliper brakes, you will
need to maintain both in good operating order.

Having taken care of the mechanics of your bike, you
are ready once more to consider riding it. It must fit you
properly if you hope to get the best performance from it.
You fit the bike to your size by moving the saddle up or
down. Generally, the saddle is set at a height that enables
you barely to get both feet flat on the ground while strad-
dling it. This allows you to flex your legs and ankles properly when you pedal. However, many prefer a lower saddle
position. It is really up to the individual; what works best

Every BMXer has a favorite seat height. This is a typically comfortable extension.

for you is best. Once the saddle is where you want it, tighten the seat clamp to prevent it from twisting or allowing the post to slip down into the tube.

You will want to adjust the handlebars to the most comfortable height in order to put the least strain on your hands and arms. Keep the handlebars fairly close and low so you don't have to reach far out or up to them. But be sure to position them so that when you turn sharply your inside elbow doesn't dig into your ribs. Also, you must have the handlebars set so they do not interfere with your churning knees.

A good set of pads helps prevent injuries.

Check your protective bike pads. Be sure they are properly secured in place along the top tube, on the handlebar cross brace, and over the protruding gooseneck. Those pads can save you a lot of misery, whether you are racing or doing fancy freestyle capers on your bike.

Now look your machine over carefully. If everything is clean and properly adjusted, if there is no grinding or rattling, you've got a bicycle you can be proud of.

It is time to start riding.

SIX

Rad Riding

Most owners of bicycles, even BMX bikes, do use their vehicles primarily to tour around the neighborhood, pedal to school, or run errands. But you don't buy a stripped-down, high-performance, pedal-powered motocross machine to use in such ordinary ways. Surely you, like almost every BMX fan, have set your sights toward the day when you will take off the chain guard, remove such accessories as the kickstand and fenders, and turn it loose at some far-out and radical trickery. You also may be aiming toward entering whatever racing competition is available in your area.

But BMX racing is a very specialized activity that demands the utmost cycling skill. Before you get into racing you should learn all you can about your bike, finding out what you can expect from it and what you can do with it. You must develop new techniques and update old riding habits. You must also practice until you learn to squeeze

66

the most pleasure and the best, but safest, performance out of your sliding, jumping, and flying machine.

This informal freestyle thrashing around with your BMX bike is sometimes called styling. If you want to describe it in a more common term, it is hotdogging. There is really nothing wrong with showing off a little on your bike, as long as you know what you are doing and don't overdo it. It is, in fact, about the best way there is to become an expert at handling your frisky BMX vehicle. Besides, it is a lot of fun.

So, start working on a few of the more exciting and exotic techniques of BMX bike riding. It is important, of course, that your bike is a BMX-style machine. The tricks that you put it through would quickly turn a normal thin-tired, gear-shifting touring bicycle into a pile of trash.

To start with, you should have little trouble doing simple wheelies with your compact bike. You merely shift your body weight rearward as you hoist up on the handlebars. Do it with rhythm and coordination. Once your front wheel is up off the ground, try to hold it at the point of balance and not topple over backward. However, if you feel yourself starting to lose control, get one or both feet down on the ground quickly. Flex your knees to soften the landing. Then try again.

To do a wheelie,
shift your body
weight rearward
while hoisting up
on the handlebars.

Soon you will find that wheelies are old stuff. You progressively increase the power you put into them. Before long you will find yourself pedaling all over the place with the front wheel as high as your head and your machine turned into a veritable unicycle.

When you become that adept at balancing on one wheel, try locking your rear coaster brake and, with only one foot on a pedal, hopping around on the rear tire as though you were on a pogo stick. This is radical riding, and it all leads toward perfecting your skills at handling your trickworthy bike. (If your bike has caliper brakes, forget this trick.)

A freestyler hopping around on one wheel.

You might also try a reverse wheelie, called an endo. Pick something like a curb, fence, or one of those concrete wheel bumpers in a parking lot to act as a wheel stopper. Approach it at a fairly low speed with both feet on the pedals. Just as your front wheel comes up against the barrier, heave your body upward off the seat while pushing down and forward on the handlebars. This brings your unweighted rear wheel up off the ground, while the barrier stops your bike from going any farther.

If you are moving too fast when you reach the barrier, you may do your own style of endo right over the bars. If you start to lose control, get your feet back to the ground

Not a crash but a fence endo.

to break the fall. However, if you do it right, suddenly you find yourself balanced precariously over the front wheel. Hold yourself there for as long as you can.

If you have a front-wheel caliper brake you can do an endo out in the open without having to use a wheel stopper. At a fairly low speed, squeeze the brake lever enough to lock the wheel while shifting your weight a little to the rear as though ready to spring. Then quickly rock up and forward to unweight the rear wheel. While pushing on the handlebars with stiffened arms, jackknife your body, shifting your rear end over the uplifting wheel. Keep your brake locked and try to stop your motion at the balance point. This so-called front-brake endo is tricky but worth mastering. When you do the maneuver correctly, you can keep both feet on the pedals; or if you want to be a little more radical, shoot your feet out in spread-eagle fashion. But get them back to the pedals as you feel the rear wheel starting to drop back to the ground. Flex your knees to soften the landing.

Next find some fairly soft dirt or sand and learn to corner and skid your bike. When it comes to racing, skillful cornering is a lot more important than skidding, for the loss of traction during a skid usually slows you down. When cornering, you should try to keep both feet working the pedals to maintain speed. Rather than skidding, try to lean into the corner to keep your tires firmly on the ground. Learn just how fast you can go into a corner and how far you can lean without putting the bike into a skid. If you are right-handed, practice more right turns, since it is really the less natural direction. Right-handers usually are more comfortable banking to the left. Vice versa if you are left-handed.

(Left) Try to keep your feet on the pedals during a turn.

(Below) On an unbanked turn, or sweeper, you can lower your inside foot for stability.

On a BMX bike frame the crank hanger is usually set high enough off the ground so that you can keep pedaling while you bank sharply into a turn without digging a pedal into the dirt. However, if you start to lose it and feel your rear wheel begin to skid out from under you, forget about both feet on the pedals. Lower your inside foot toward the ground to catch yourself. Remember to keep your outside, or upside, foot pushing hard on that pedal. This not only helps keep you in control but brings the inside pedal up high off the ground and out of danger.

Try some deliberate skids. Force your bike over on its side and turn your handlebars until the rear wheel begins to slide out from under you. Recover by turning the handlebars in the direction of the skid, and bend your body upward to keep downward pressure on the tires. Cornering and skidding are great fun. They also teach you important aspects of controlling your bike.

Try some panic stops. Accelerate to a good speed, then lock your brake and bring your bike to a controlled skidding stop. If you start to crash, release the brake to regain balance.

Those are a few ground maneuvers that will help you become better acquainted with your BMX machine. However, once you have become a confirmed BMXer, you will

Skidding is fun but not speed producing.

have the overwhelming desire to make your bike fly. This involves all kinds of jumps and the contortions that go with them.

To get the feel of antigravity maneuvers, or "taking air" as it is called, start with some simple feats of wheels-up bicycle hopping. Do not begin by tackling some unresisting concrete curb; start by trying to hop over some crushable object. Make it a small cardboard carton, a pile of old newspapers, or anything soft enough to absorb errors.

Lower your body as you approach the object at medium coasting speed. Keep your pedals level and both feet solidly on them. A bike length or so before you reach the barrier, begin shifting your weight upward off the saddle while you pull the front end up into the start of a wheelie. As you are about to crash into the obstacle, slide back over the rear wheel and, with a coordinated rolling motion, bend your knees and push forward and down on the handlebars. This brings the unweighted rear wheel up. When you get the proper rhythm, you will become airborne and sail right over the object. You need only flex your knees to soften the landing. With practice, you will find yourself soaring over ever higher barricades.

Having mastered the basic knack of flight through shifting body movement, you can start thinking about high-

In jumping, slide back off the seat to bring the front wheel up, then push down on the handlebars to lower the front wheel and bring the rear wheel up and over the hump.

speed jumping, which is used in performing freestyle tricks and is also part of BMX racing. Look for natural humps or bumps that have good approach paths, or dig out some old lumber and nail together a practice ramp. Just be sure the ramp is strong enough and not too steep or high. Eighteen to twenty-four inches is a nice starting height for a ramp. Have some fairly soft landing dirt beyond its high end.

In this type of jumping, speed is essential. Without sufficient momentum you will either go *thud* off the end of the ramp or, even worse, have your front wheel drop and catapult you over the handlebars in a painful header. So take the ramp with a good head of steam. On your first jumps you can stop pedaling just before you take to the air. Concentrate on shifting your weight rearward off the saddle to keep the back wheel lower than the front wheel, thus avoiding the possibility of landing front wheel first and being hurtled over the handlebars.

Just don't get your rear wheel down so fast that you risk flipping over backward or losing time in the air. Once in midair, press against your handlebars just enough to bring the front wheel back down, but not below the level of your rear wheel. You must tilt your bike so you land rear wheel first. Ideally, it should touch down an instant before the front wheel. If you do land on the front wheel and don't

Jumping off a ramp is good practice for taking air.

have solid straight-ahead steering control, you will almost surely flop. As always, absorb the shock of landing with an overall flexing of your body and limbs.

This is a good time to establish the important fact that speed jumping is more for show than go. As you will find out when you begin to race, the best way to maintain racing speed is to keep the tires on the ground, not in the air. You will always lose some speed and possibly even control when your wheels are off the ground, not churning on the track.

As you improve your riding and jumping skills as well as your physical stamina, you can add a few fancy touches if you like. You probably will try soaring off ever higher bumps or ramps. You will try some cross-ups—instead of keeping your front wheel pointed forward in preparation for the landing, twist your handlebars sharply at a ninety-degree angle while you are still in flight. This, of course, turns the front wheel sideways to your direction of travel and looks pretty impressive. Be sure that you have enough time and airspace to turn the wheel back to its forward heading before you reach the ground; otherwise you will wipe out.

As you become ever more adept at freestyling and find yourself soaring ever higher, you might want to do a trick called a tabletop. You need plenty of speed and a good

(Left) Taking air
and doing cross-ups
is more for show
than for go.

(Below) The flat-out
tabletop is one of
the most dramatic
freestyle maneuvers.

ramp to get you airborne. At the height of your jump, when you are four feet or so in the air, wrench your handlebars over sharply and push out sideways with your legs and body. This lays the bike out horizontally in midair. Positioned in this way, you could almost set your machine with dishes and silverware. But again, you must return to a vertical position and get your wheels under you before hitting the ground. It's a spectacular but risky trick, as are most aerial stunts, and you should be an expert biker before you try it.

There are many other tricks you can do on your BMX bike, such as riding backward on the handlebars, or balancing your bike by standing on the front wheel. Or you can do a 180-degree turn by riding up an embankment, planting a foot on the ground, then twirling the bike in a wide arc up over your head, bringing it down pointing in the opposite direction, vaulting back on, and riding off.

New and exciting tricks are being tried out every day by daredevil cyclists with inventive minds. You should try whatever is reasonably safe and whatever you feel you are capable of performing. Thrashing about with no particular purpose other than having fun is certain to improve your skillfulness with your bike. But the wise biker doesn't overstep his or her talents, ignore safety, or do damage to an expensive machine.

(Left) Riding backward has no practical purpose, but it does help you master your bike.

(Below) Twirling the bike over your head then jumping on and riding away in the opposite direction is another trick you can learn.

Also, although informal trick riding on a BMX bike is all part of the excitement of the new style of riding, it is only a small part of actual BMX action. There is a great deal of difference between freestyle trickery and actual bicycle motocross racing.

Leave this kind of freestyling to the pros.

SEVEN

Ready to Race

The day will come when you feel ready to go out and test your riding skills against the racers in your area. To find out more about the competitive side of this sport, you might do some inquiring first. Talk to some of the other BMXers in your neighborhood. Find out where you can go to watch some actual races. Learn what official BMX competition is all about. See if there are any rulebooks at your local bike shop.

To have any real fun you need to be with other bikers who are interested in motocross action. Join a BMX racing club. If one does not already exist, get several riders together and form one. Again, bike-shop owners usually are happy to help and may even offer the use of part of the shop for a meeting place.

You may have to publicize. Post a notice on your school bulletin board. Try to convince a local newspaper to run a feature article on some aspects of bicycle moto-

A car carrier gets bikes to the track.

cross. And keep talking to anyone you happen to see thrashing around on his or her bike. Before you know it, there will be a group of friends and new acquaintances eager to test their motocross racing skills on an official BMX track.

There are many different groups and organizations involved or willing to become involved in BMX racing. Some have only local interests. Others have statewide concerns. Then there are those national sanctioning bodies such as the NBL, ABA, and NBA, whose rules and regulations are not always the same but who are making efforts to standardize the codes and restrictions of BMX competition.

There are various methods of putting a racing schedule

together. The meet usually is planned by a group of adult sponsors who are aided by officials from a bicycle motocross organization, as well as by helpful counsel from a few of the area's more experienced riders.

Important to any racing meet is the method for awarding points and trophies. This, too, varies widely from track to track and meet to meet. A rider should check with the officials to learn whatever system is being used for that day's competition. Trophies are nice to have over the fireplace, but it is the gathering of points that usually accompany the trophies that enables a BMXer to move upward in class from novice to expert. With enough points, and the fame that sometimes goes with them, he or she might even get the chance to turn pro. But it takes a lot of hard work and dedication, plus doing well in local, state, regional, and, indeed, national BMX race meets to earn a spot near or at the top.

Whoever garners enough first-, second-, or third-place finishes and collects a sufficient number of award points earns the privilege of displaying the number "1" on the bicycle's racing plate. This means that the cyclist is best in the class—at least until the next season when the point gathering starts again and the scramble for number 1 begins anew.

If you aspire to racing in official BMX meets, you must

abide by whatever rules apply to the particular time and place the event is being held. Even though regulations vary from meet to meet, there are a few standard rules that apply to any track. For instance, you must register beforehand and probably pay a small entry fee. You must be willing to have a technical inspection of your bike in order to be sure that it is safe and properly adjusted. You must be ready to take your position in the starting gate when the race is called, or lose your turn. If you try to leave the starting gate too soon, you will be disqualified. During the race you cannot leave the track or cut corners in order to gain an advantage. However, if you are crowded off the track or have to dodge around a crash, you are permitted to get back on the track to finish the race.

You cannot deliberately push or kick an opponent or use foul language without being disqualified. In fact, the basic rules of racing deal largely with practicing good sportsmanship at all times.

Generally, rules dictate that you compete within your own age group. Also the amount of racing experience you have had is often taken into account. However, if there are not enough registrants in any single group to fill all the slots, usually between four and eight, at the starting gate, groups are frequently combined to make a race. After all,

BMX riding often starts at a tender age.

there's not apt to be a great deal of difference in skill between, say, a nine-year-old and a ten-year-old.

Open competition provides you with the opportunity to pit your techniques against older, although not necessarily better, riders. Here you may even find yourself racing against a professional in open pro-am competition.

Most BMX races are run on sixteen- or twenty-inch wheel bikes. However, some of the older and bigger racers, including a few adults who enter special races, ride larger twenty-four- and twenty-six-inch open-wheel cruiser-class bicycles. All bikes compete on the same track,

Relatives are needed in official roles.

but one size does not race against the other. Also, sons, daughters, and parents may race in the same meet although not against each other in the same events.

Nonriding relatives are needed to help out in various officiating chores. They serve in such capacities as starters, judges, scorekeepers, and track marshalls. This type of participation helps to make bicycle motocross a fun family affair.

Having familiarized yourself with the rules, consider the track—a very important item, indeed. If a motocross track already exists within a reasonable distance, you have no real problem. If not, you may have to try getting one built. Again, this means getting adults involved. An organization that has an interest in youth projects is a likely source of aid, both physical and financial. Service clubs and non-profit organizations such as the Kiwanis, Lions, Rotary, or Jaycees can be very helpful in getting a track established. The scouts, the Y's, the police and fire departments, and the local parks and recreation organization can provide valuable support. Often they can arrange for the use of land on which to build a track and even for the dirt-moving equipment usually needed for construction. Before approaching civic and municipal organizations, however, you should get yourselves organized; and a BMX club is the way.

A BMX racetrack may be a simple affair with a few handy obstacles to challenge the cyclists. Or it can be a complicated and expensive layout, carefully planned, surveyed, constructed, and maintained. It all depends on how successful you and your group have been in getting parents, friends, and the community interested in sponsoring BMX-racing competition.

Approximately an acre and a half to three acres of ground is needed to construct a decent track. This also allows space for parking, bleachers, a snack stand, restrooms, and other facilities necessary for a successful program. The land needn't be level. However, if it is slanted

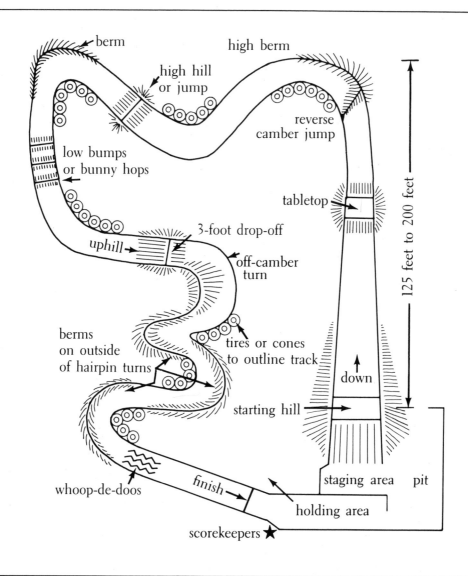

berm

high berm

high hill
or jump

reverse
camber jump

low bumps
or bunny hops

125 feet to 200 feet

tabletop

3-foot drop-off

uphill

off-camber
turn

berms
on outside
of hairpin turns

tires or cones
to outline track

down

starting hill

whoop-de-doos

finish

staging area   pit

holding area

scorekeepers ★

A track layout allows for numerous obstacles.

Indoor as well as outdoor tracks are popular.

or rolling, the track should be laid out so the starting gate is on high ground and the finish line at a low spot. A downhill run makes for a faster race. It enables the racers to build up speed as the race progresses and is much easier on the legs than having to pedal uphill.

A downward-slanting track also is suitable for another exciting event featured in some race meets—racing side hacks. A side hack is simply a bike with a sidecar added. It becomes a two-man vehicle, with one working the pedals while the other rides the sidecar and tries to maintain balance around the curves and over the jumps. Somewhat heavy machines, the side hacks really need this type of track in order to build up and maintain speed.

Side hacks are fun on trail or track.

Any officially sanctioned track has basic similarities. These include assorted time-tested features designed to challenge the competitors' racing skills. Ideally, the starting hill should be approximately twenty-four feet wide in order to accommodate a field of eight racers, although many fine tracks can handle only about six starters at a time. If there is no natural high point, a mound should be shoveled or bulldozed several feet higher than the rest of the track.

The starting gate is the all-important beginning of any track. A few small tracks simply drop a stretched-out rope to start a race. Some tracks have electronic or other extravagant starting gates. The most common and inexpensive one, though, is a long hinged plank laid across the starting

An elevated starting ramp is important to any BMX track.

ramp. Tilted on edge, the plank effectively blocks the front wheels. At the end of the countdown the starter throws a lever that drops the plank flush to the ground and sets the bikes free.

Below the starting ramp is a straightaway over which cyclists can build up speed before reaching the first turn. Since contestants begin to string out along that first straight, the track narrows somewhat. To add interest most tracks place some kind of a jump on the way to the first curve.

There are several additional turns along the winding track. Some, called sweepers, may be so flat that riders have to cut back sharply on speed to prevent their bikes from skidding out beneath them. Or a curve may even be

The fastest turns are banked, or bermed.

off camber, or banked slightly to the outside. Such a curve requires extreme care in order to keep the tire treads biting the ground and holding the track.

The most common and exciting turn is a high-speed inside banked corner protected by a curving wall of dirt called a berm. Any track should have both right- and left-hand corners in order to test contestants' ability to maneuver in both directions.

Beyond each curve there is usually a straight section of track, allowing cyclists to build back their momentum after being slowed down in the corners. However, the straights are not always simple level stretches. Not only do they vary in length, but they are usually interrupted by some kind of a jump or drop-off. Somewhere enroute contestants may have to pick their way through a field of moguls, or anthills. These are a bunch of small dirt mounds sprinkled along the way and meant to rattle teeth and shake bikes apart.

Some tracks even have water jumps or, worse still, mud pits. The latter have lost much of their popularity, not only because they make a mess of shoes and clothes, but because they are equally rough on bikes. Mud clogs wheels, bearings, chains, and other parts that must be kept clean and in good operating condition. Another challenging jump is the tabletop. It may be several feet high, with a broad flat top that drops off sharply at its far edge.

A ramp leads to an elevated tabletop.

Somewhere along the final third of their length, most tracks add a series of three closely spaced jumps called whoop-de-doos, or simply whoops. They form a veritable roller coaster and present a real challenge. The BMXer has to decide whether to take them one at a time, to leap the first two and hope not to crash onto the third, or if he or she has built up sufficient speed, to try to clear them all in one super jump. How this jump is handled probably will differ from track to track and depend upon that day's conditions.

A track usually will present a final challenge along the last straightaway to the finish line. This tests the competitors' muscles and spirit to determine if they have anything left after about a half minute of agonizing strain over a punishing course that twists and turns for an overall length of between seven hundred and nine hundred feet.

The finish line itself might be a rope stretched across the dirt, or a line of banners strung overhead, or almost anything that will allow the judges to determine the order of finishes.

Spills, of course, are commonplace on any BMX track. It is part of the fun, although it also can be part of the pain. So a track must be equipped with certain safeguards. Many tracks are bordered with used tires that not only help guide the cyclists but provide a fairly soft crash landing for

Crashes are commonplace.

those going out of control. Hay bales also are used as protective barriers adjacent to jumps, berms, and whoop-de-
doos. Other than such built-in comforts, however, a rider
will generally rely on the softness of the dirt to cushion
any falls.

You need to take care of several things before you can
enter a race. Generally you don't need to belong to a
BMX organization if you enter beginners' events or even
often race in the novice class. But you surely will want to
work your way upward. And, in order to race in the expert
class or open events, you need to be a member of a race-

sanctioning organization, whether local, statewide, or national. Different sanctioning bodies have varied requirements, although they all fit a basic pattern. If you join one of the larger BMX organizations, you are given a competition card with your name, address, age, and designation—beginner, novice, expert, or professional—on it. You are also issued an identification number so that your records can be handily kept. The last two or three digits of your identification number may serve as your rider number, which goes on your bicycle plate in about six-inch-high numerals. An initial, such as the first letter of your last name, may be added for even more precise identification. At some of the larger meets, such as the Nationals, you usually are issued a separate new number when you register and pay your fee. It applies only to that meet, and chances are you get a new one-time number plate to go with it.

As with so many things in the rapidly growing sport of BMX racing, the issuing of racing numbers often varies. So you must inquire into and abide by whatever system exists at the time.

Your club dues should provide you with a full year's paid-up racing insurance, and you usually receive some kind of monthly newsletter. Also, the organization you

Only a few BMX racers earn a single-digit racing-plate number.

join maintains a record of the points you earn at properly sanctioned race meets. This provides you with some measure by which you can compare your racing prowess to that of other contestants. Also, as you progress from beginner upward, the card is marked to show your current class rating.

By the time race day arrives you should be pretty well prepared. You belong to one of the regional or national sponsoring organizations as well as to your local club. When you arrive at the track that day, you register and pay a small fee for whatever individual races, or motos, you choose to enter. You are issued a number to go on your racing plate. When you become good enough to rate a single digit, such as 1, 2, 3, or so on, you will have joined the BMX motocrossing elite.

Part of the registration fee goes toward purchasing trophies and helping to defray expenses of operating the track. Most important, however, it gets you a position at the starting gate.

Once you have registered, you usually are free to take a couple of preliminary spins around the track and get the feel of it and of your bike. This allows you to see what you will be getting into so that you can set up some plan of how to attack the track and run your best race. Of course, many unsuspected factors will conspire to upset your ideas, but you should have a plan to start with.

Well before official race time you should take your bike into the pit and do whatever adjusting and setting up you think might help you in the race. Try to get it done before an official comes by to give you the required safety inspection. Tighten everything properly. Check your tire pressures. If the track is hardpacked, you might want to keep the pressure down to thirty-five or forty pounds per square inch (p.s.i.) so the rubber holds to the surface. On a soft track try forty-five or even fifty p.s.i., since you need the extra firmness to keep your wheels from mushing in the loose dirt or sand.

Also consider your gear ratio. Remember that a hard gear ratio (large chainwheel, small rear sprocket) provides more revolutions of the wheel with each turn of the pedals but requires more muscle power. Soft gearing (smaller chainwheel, larger rear sprocket) gets you out of the gate quickly and pulls better through loose dirt. However, you have to spin the pedals faster in order to maintain speed on a straightaway. The choice is yours, providing you have several extra chainwheels and sprockets from which to choose. If you don't have a choice of gear ratios—many bikes come with nonchangeable or hard-to-change sprock-

(Above) Get your bike race-ready in the pit.

(Right) Check tire pressure.

ets, front and rear—you will have to do your best with what you have.

Clean and lubricate your bike as you see fit. When you feel that you have your machine in topnotch racing condition, go over and check the moto sheets for the scheduling of the first moto in which you are entered. See what time it starts and which moto you follow. Learn what position in the starting gate you have drawn. If you discover that you have drawn one of the inside positions, you have reason to be at least temporarily happy. An inside position gives you a slight advantage during the all-out battle to the first turn.

When you return to the pit you may find an official busily inspecting those bikes about to go racing. If you have done your work, you can feel confident that your bike is completely trackworthy.

The inspector seems to agree. But he also checks your personal gear—sturdy helmet, long-sleeved shirt, proper shoes and socks. He seems concerned about your rather loose pant legs. You slip a couple of rubber bands over your right leg to prevent the fabric from catching in the unguarded chain and sprocket. Then, since there is no protection built into your pants, you strap on knee pads. Before he can suggest it, you dig two elbow pads out of

Just waiting for the action to start.

your equipment bag and slip them on as well.

"Be sure to tighten your chin strap good and firm when you get ready to race," he cautions. Then he pats you on the shoulder. "Good luck," he says, and leaves.

You feel the tension building up inside. You take a deep breath and try to relax.

"I'm ready," you tell yourself confidently. "Let's get going!"

EIGHT

The Race

Under the trees and out of the heat, the staging area is chock-full of stripped down, knobby-tired BMX bikes and nervous riders. It's a big meet, one of the many Nationals held each year in different parts of the country. And during the season you've earned enough award points in local, state, and regional meets to get you there.

From the direction of the bleachers the crowd noise swells and subsides as one moto after another is run off. From the staging area you cannot see what race is underway, but the upwelling roar of the fans tells you that the racers are charging toward the checkered flag. As the sound dwindles, you see exhausted racers off to your right skid to a dusty stop on the short track overrun beyond the finish line.

Two of the finishers grin and shake hands. Another rips off his hclmct and slams it to the ground. He'd better watch out, you think, or a judge will cite him for unsportsmanlike conduct.

The staging area is crowded with eager racers.

By virtue of the transfer system the three or four who finished first have qualified to move on to a more advanced moto later on in the meet. The helmet thrower will have to await another day and another meet, using the time to learn better control over his bike and his temper.

You fidget astride your bike and wait for your race number to be called over the loudspeaker. You have already taken third place in your first moto, which was run off before noon. Not great but good enough to transfer you up a notch and into the quarterfinals. Then in the quarters you were running a poor fifth and pretty much out of contention when the number-two rider made a frantic effort to take the lead. He was almost abreast of the leader when his

Everyone tries to relax between motos.

right pedal caught in his opponent's wheel. Both racers went down in a tangle of frayed spokes. You dodged around the melee and crossed the line with another third. It was good enough to get you into the semis. It also built up your point standing a little and increased your chances for a trophy. You feel good about this day. Already you have gained a bit in your national ranking. If you can keep it up, if you can make it to the main event, or mains, who knows, you may be well on your way to earning one of those much coveted single-digit numbers for your handlebar plate.

Having checked the moto sheet, you are satisfied to have drawn the number-three position in the gate. Not bad for a field of eight. At least you stand a fair chance of getting an inside line to the first turn.

You hear your race number called. You and seven other contestants walk your bikes out past the other riders who are gathered in the staging area waiting for their own races. An official checks you through, and you push your bike up the ramp leading to the elevated starting gate.

You settle your bike into the number-three slot and brace your front wheel up against the tilted plank. You look forward and draw a deep breath, just as you've done the other two times you set yourself up in that gate. It must be fifteen or more feet high, with the track falling sharply out in front of you. Once the gate goes down, it's going to be like dropping off a wall. But what a way to get off to a fast start.

"Get your wheel against the gate," the starter prompts the rider two slots to your right. Soon all bikes are in place.

You straddle the seat, supporting yourself with one foot on the ground and the other up on the high pedal ready to push down when the gate drops. You try to relax, but there is no way. You breathe deeply to calm your nerves, and prepare for the countdown. You hear the expectant murmur of the crowd as they await the start. You feel that all eyes are on you and gulp self-consciously.

"Riders ready," the starter calls.

You try to remember what his cadence was during your other two starts earlier in the day. You must time it just right in order to break from the gate the instant the plank drops. If you start too soon, your front wheel will be blocked an extra moment against the gate. If you are a split second late, the other riders will get off to an early lead.

"Pedals set!"

You lift your foot from the ground and settle it on the other pedal. You balance there, both feet up, for a two-pedal start. For a frantic moment you fear you may have misjudged the starter's cadence and that you will lose your balance and have to drop one foot back to the ground. You lean back a little. Call it. Call it! you mentally implore the starter.

"Go!"

The starter drops the gate lever. Immediately the long hinged plank flops forward flush to the ground, suddenly releasing the front wheels of all eight bikes.

You snap your weight forward and push hard on your high pedal. But you temper the pressure slightly with your other foot to keep the rear wheel from spinning ineffectively in the dirt.

Your tire holds its grip, and as you accelerate steeply

(Left) In the gate.

(Below) The gate
goes down.

downward, you are elated to discover that you got the best
start, the hole shot. You reach the bottom of the ramp
slightly ahead of the field.

But your joy is short-lived. Halfway down the first
straightaway you somehow slip a pedal. Before you can get
your foot back on and regain momentum, two riders surge
past. The trouble worsens when, going over the first low
jump, you soar too high, taking too much air, as BMXers
say, and still another racer slips past you on the inside.

Off to a good start.

You scold yourself for not staying low and keeping your rubber on the ground and churning. Taking air may look good to the fans, but being airborne slows you down. Of course, you will take some air on any jump, but the idea is to get your bike back down on the ground as quickly as possible, since you cannot pedal and accelerate with your wheels in the air. "Remember," you tell yourself, "air for show; down for go!"

You approach the first left-hand turn in fourth place. It's a reverse camber turn, banked slightly from the inside of the curve to the outside. As you go into it you touch your brake lever to slow down a little so your momentum won't send you skidding off and into the bordering straw

Over a bump together.

bales. But you brake a little too much, lose traction—and another rider slips past.

You fight back rising panic and thrust harder on the pedals, trying desperately to make up the yards you have lost. You sense another bike is directly behind you, but you dare not glance back. Looking over your shoulder is a sure way to lose that split second it takes for the pursuing rider to pass you. Eyes ahead.

Pedaling hard, you take a center line as you weave through a steeply banked S-turn. You hear a crash and a loud yelp behind you as someone goes down. But you are not even tempted to look back. The race is ahead, not behind.

Don't look back. What you see may discourage you.

You approach a second and higher jump. The number-four racer appears to misjudge its height. He pulls a wheelie to help the front end of his bike up and over, but he goes too far and nearly loops it. You hunch over your bike and pedal furiously. You pull your front wheel up over the jump, then push down on the handlebars and shift your weight rearward over the back wheel to get it down to the ground. You take some air but not much, and you land smoothly and pointed straight ahead. Before the other racer can regain equilibrium, you spurt back into fourth place.

Taking air over a jump.

You are settling into position just off the rear wheel of
the number-three bike when the next turn looms ahead. It
is protected by a high-banking berm. You size up the action in front, trying to decide whether to go high onto the
berm or stay low. Going low is the shortest route through
the curve, and the other three bikes battle for the inside
position. But the turn is a sharp one and they go into it so
fast that each has to take an inside foot off the pedal and
slide it along the ground to support himself when his bike
begins to skid. As the three bikes start skidding and throw-
ing up a spray of dirt, you decide suddenly to take the
longer route around the turn. You steer your way high up
on the berm, keeping both feet on the pedals and cranking
for all you are worth. The number-three rider makes a
tactical error; he glances over his left shoulder to see how
close you are. But you are not there, having swung high
up onto the berm. And you make your move. Halfway
through the turn, you cut sharply down and across the
face of the berm and spurt past one surprised rider. By the
time he recovers and gets both feet back on the pedals, you
are two yards in front and trying to close on the other two
riders racing almost wheel to wheel down the straightaway
toward the five-foot-high mound of a tabletop jump.

Your legs ache, and a clod of damp earth kicked up by
someone's wheel slams against your visor, momentarily

Go high up on the berm in order to cut down ahead
of the low riders.

blinding you. You shake it off just in time to see the leader
lift his front wheel for the jump up onto the tabletop. He
is going too fast and takes too much air. By the time he
comes down onto the flat surface and gets his machine
squared away, the second rider overtakes him.

You vault your own bike up the steep incline, take air,
quickly shift your weight back over the rear wheel, and get
it back on the ground. You keep the pedals churning
across the flat surface until suddenly you are looking into
the open space just before the sheer drop-off from the high
tabletop.

Tired and aching as you are, you scarcely note what is happening ahead. It seems, though, that the leader already has landed roughly at the base of the drop-off and is struggling to regain full control of his bike. You are aware, too, that the second-place bike is in midair, with its front wheel dipping dangerously low.

As you power your way across the short tabletop and come to the drop-off, you hoist your handlebars up and again shift your weight rearward over the back wheel to bring it down before the front wheel. You become airborne. You struggle to hold your balance and keep the front wheel aimed straight ahead. You land a mere wheel length behind the second-place racer. You make a smooth landing. He had come down with a jolt and slipped a pedal. You put extra power to the cranks while he is still busily trying to get a flailing foot back on his pedal.

As you churn up beside him, your rival flashes you a panicky look. Then he swerves in on you and deliberately tries to crowd you into the tires bordering the straightaway. He's clever, and you doubt that the track marshalls have noticed the foul.

As he closes in, you ward him off with a knee and elbow. It's perfectly legal; you are allowed to defend your position. You slip on past, paying no attention to his shouts.

The drop-off from a tabletop.

You are two-thirds through the course, and the ache settles deeper into your back and limbs. You suck in all the air you can get to supply oxygen to run your muscle machinery. You start to close gradually on the leader. Appreciating the drama, the crowd roars encouragement.

Up ahead the late afternoon shadows slanting across the whoop-de-doos make them look like three closely spaced miniature mountain ranges. Staying just inside the leader's rear wheel, you wonder what he plans to do. Will he slow a bit, keep his rear wheel close to the ground, and take the whoops one at a time? Or will he make the giant leap and try to soar over all three whoops at once? During your earlier races you had decided that the whoops were spread out too far to take in one flying leap. But now, as you continue to build up speed, you begin to dislike the idea of slowing down and bunny-hopping over them individually.

Then you see that the leader is doing just that. After all, it's the safer and more controlled way to maneuver these obstacles. Besides, he has the lead and needs only to hold it a little longer. He eases up a bit on his cranks so he won't hit the first jump at a speed that will launch him into the air but will still let him keep his rear wheel churning on the ground.

And now you make your decision. It's a risk, but a reasonable one if you hope to win the race. Ten yards from the nearest whoop you forget the ache in your legs and put all of your flagging strength into the pedals. Going at high speed, you fly off the top of the first mound and keep on sailing. For a moment you fear that you have misjudged and that your front wheel will crash into the near side of the second whoop and wipe you out completely. But you continue to sail, and the front wheel barely clears the second mound. You shift your weight forward, pushing down on the handlebars to bring the back wheel up and over.

Taking the whoop-de-doos.

Then you thrust your rear out over the back wheel to force it to the ground first.

Having successfully cleared two of the whoops in one leap, you hit the ground just short of the third mound. The jarring crash to earth dislodges a foot. You get it back on the pedal just in time to crank your way over the third one.

Your daring maneuver has brought you handlebar to handlebar with your rival. You can't see him, but you know he is beside you, breathing hard and grunting over the pedals. Straight ahead looms another berm-protected turn. It is not quite as sharp or high as the others but still a real test for your waning strength.

You think of again going high onto the berm and trying to charge downward out into the lead. But you don't feel that you have that much power left in your legs. So you take the inside line. So does your equally tired opponent. As the two of you race wheel to wheel, your bikes clash together momentarily. It is part of racing and neither rider's fault. But in breaking apart, your opponent lets his bike drift a little toward the outside. You fight to hold your line going into the final straightaway. With about fifty yards to go, you race wheel to wheel.

There is nothing left in your legs. And there is still one

more jump ahead. A nagging little imp sits on your shoulder and tells you to forget it. Settle for second. But you have heard that faceless voice before. You've never listened, and you don't intend to now. You stand on the pedals and *pump, pump, pump.* You no longer feel the ache. Just a numbness . . . and determination.

Then you are at the final jump. Don't lose it now. Up with the front wheel, then forward on the handlebars and weight back to get the rear wheel down on the ground. Good. The rear wheel comes down smoothly with the knobby rubber biting into the dirt.

But your opponent is still beside you, giving his all. You duck low, and, standing on the pedals, keep cranking. The finish line looms ahead. You lean your weight a little farther forward over the handlebars. Then, a bare yard before the finish line you snap your body upright and your legs forward, thrusting your bike almost out from under you, and across the line. When you hit the brake, you skid to a stop on the short stretch of overrun.

The other fellow also skids to a stop. He grins over at you. Does he think he won? You don't think so. You believe you made it with that final thrust. You wait for the signal from the judges, and the announcement over the loudspeaker.

A final sprint to the finish.

And somehow, for the moment, it doesn't seem all that important who really won. It was a terrific race. First or second place, you have qualified for entry in the finals . . . the mains. Another chance to race. And that's what really counts, the racing. Only the racing!

berm—dirt bank on a turn.

bottom bracket—short tube at bottom of bicycle frame into which crank axle and bearings fit.

brake arm—curved clamplike arm to which brake shoe is attached.

brake lever—part mounted on handlebars that activates caliper brake.

brake shoe—pad that provides friction braking against wheel.

caliper brake—hand-operated brake.

chain stays—sections of bicycle frame from bottom bracket to rear wheel drop-outs.

chainwheel—large pedal-powered front sprocket.

chrome-moly—high-grade chrome-molybdenum steel.

coaster brake—foot-activated brake in rear hub of bicycle.

cog—rear sprocket.

crank—metal rotating arm to which pedal is attached.

crash and burn—to take a spill.

cross-up—to turn front wheel sideways in midair.

dirt riding—offroad riding on paths or trails.

down tube—part of bicycle frame reaching from steering head to bottom bracket.

drive train—power-producing assembly of pedals, sprockets, chain, and rear wheel.

drop-off—steep drop in the track.

drop-outs—axle slots in forks and stays.

endo—reverse wheelie, tipping forward on front wheel. Also an end-over-end spill.

factory team—group of sponsored riders.

flat sweep—turn that is not bermed. Also called *sweeper*.

freestyle—innovative or trick riding. Also called *styling*.

freewheel—brakeless, toothed rear sprocket. Cog.

front fork—pivoting steering assembly holding front wheel.

gooseneck—clamp that holds handlebars. Also called *stem*.

gusset—metal tab welded at corners of frame to reinforce it.

hack—sidecar attached to BMX bicycle. Also called *side hack*.

hardtail—early term given to BMX bikes not having spring suspension system for absorbing shock.

head—front of frame. Also called *steering head*.

headset—bearing assembly in steering head tube.

hole shot—first competitor out of the starting gate.

hub—center part of wheel holding spokes, bearings, and axle.

knobby—tire with large traction knobs on tread.

lay it down—to make a flat, low, corner skid.

main—final race in a class; main event.

meet—program of racing events.

moto—single race or preliminary heat.

pit—area near track set aside for preparation or repairing of bikes.

powder puffs—girl riders. Also BMX events specifically for females.

radical (Rad)—unusual riding performance. Tricky.

rake—to slant forward or back from the perpendicular.

rattrap pedals—sure-grip, caged, racing-type pedals.

rim—wheel, minus spokes and hub.

saddle—seat.

sanction—authorization for holding a meet according to established rules and regulations.

seat post—adjustable cylinder to which seat attaches.

seat stays—part of bicycle frame extending from just under seat to rear wheel axle and drop-outs.

seat tube—frame tube into which seat post slips.

side hack—sidecar attached to BMX bicycle. Also called *hack*.

slip a pedal—to jar a foot off the pedal.

speed jump—to jump and keep pedaling in midair.

spider—starlike bracket to accommodate a choice of chainwheels.

sprocket—toothed chain-driven wheel.

steering head—short forward frame tube that holds front forks and bearings. Also called *head*.

stem—clamp that holds handlebars. Also called *gooseneck*.

straights—straightaway sections of track.

styling—innovative or trick riding. Also called *freestyle*.

sweeper—flat curve. Also called *flat sweep*.

tabletop—flat-topped jump. Also the maneuver of laying bike out on side in midjump.

take air—to have bike in a position where both wheels are off the ground.

team—group of riders under single sponsor or captain.

thrashing—just goofing around on BMX bike.

top tube—generally horizontal tube on frame stretching from steering head to seat tube.

torque—getaway power.

transfer—to place high enough in one race to advance to another level.

wheelie—to ride with front wheel up off the ground.

whoop-de-doos—series of bumps in track. Also called *whoops*.

wipeout—to lose control of bike and "crash and burn."

FOR FURTHER INFORMATION

National Bicycle League (NBL)
3801 North Federal Highway
Pompano Beach, FL 33064

American Bicycle Association (ABA)
Box 718
Chandler, AZ 85224

FOR FURTHER READING

Bicycle Motocross Action Magazine
3162 Kashiwa Street
Torrance, CA 90505

Bicycles Today (Official NBL publication)
3801 North Federal Highway (Suite 8)
Pompano Beach, FL 33064

BMX *Plus* Magazine
20705 Western Avenue
Torrance, CA 90501

INDEX

References to illustrations are in **boldface**.

ABA (American Bicycle Association), viii, 8, 84
Allen screw key, 55
alloys, 17-18, 21, 22
anthills (moguls), 95
associations for bicycle riding and racing, 8, 13, 84, 97-100

backwards riding, 80, **81**
berms, **90**, **94**, 115, **116**, 121
bicycles, BMX, 17, **36**, 37
    car carrier for, **84**
    caring for, 52-65
    choosing, 35-40
    description of, 5, 15-34
    price of, 36
    weight of, 35
    See also specific parts

BMX (bicycle motocross), background and history of, 1-9
brakes, 31-**32**, 37-38
    See also caliper brakes
building a bicycle, 20
bunny hops, **90**

caliper brakes, 31-**32**, 38
    with endo, 70-71
    tuning of, 62-63
cambered turns, **90**, 94, 112-113
chains, **26**, **28**, 30-31, 39
    cleaning and tuning of, 59-61, **59**, **60**
chainwheels, 25, **26**, **28**
chrome molybdenum (chrome-moly), 17, 21
classes of BMX riders, 9-10, 86-88

Charles (Chick) Coombs graduated from the University of California, at Los Angeles, and decided at once to make writing his career. While working at a variety of jobs, he labored at his typewriter early in the morning and late at night. An athlete at school and college, Mr. Coombs began by writing sports fiction. He soon broadened his interests, writing adventure and mystery stories, and factual articles as well. When he had sold over a hundred stories, he decided to try one year of full-time writing, chiefly for young people, and the results justified the decision.

Eventually he turned to writing books. To date, he has published more than sixty books, both fiction and nonfiction, covering a wide range of subjects, from aviation, space, and oceanography, to drag racing, motorcycling, and other sports.

Mr. Coombs and his wife, Eleanor, live in Westlake Village, near Los Angeles.